WHY I AM A METHODIST

George R. Crooks

New York: Eaton & Mains; Cincinnati: Jennings & Graham

Originally published in the North American Review in 1886

CROSSREACH
PUBLICATIONS

Hope. Inspiration. Trust.

WE'RE SOCIAL! FOLLOW US FOR NEW TITLES AND DEALS:
FACEBOOK.COM/CROSSREACHPUBLICATIONS
@CROSSREACHPUB

AVAILABLE IN PAPERBACK AND EBOOK EDITIONS
PLEASE GO ONLINE FOR MORE GREAT TITLES
AVAILABLE THROUGH CROSSREACH PUBLICATIONS.
AND IF YOU ENJOYED THIS BOOK PLEASE CONSIDER LEAVING A
REVIEW ON AMAZON. THAT HELPS US OUT A LOT. THANKS.

I CANNOT better begin this article than in the words of Professor Austin Phelps, of Andover Seminary, an eminent representative of orthodox Congregationalism: "The rise of Methodism was the birth of a spiritual reform of which all the Christian denominations in Great Britain and America were in desperate need. The Established Churches of England and Scotland were dying of spiritual *anaemia*. Dr. Blair at Edinburgh and Bishop Porteous at London were droning moral platitudes in the pulpits, while the masses of the people, especially in England, never heard of them or of the gospel they professed to preach. Never before, nor since, has the phenomenon been so signally developed, of Christianity gasping in the struggle to live on the religion of nature. Among the ruling classes religious convictions had no intensity, and religious life no reality. The chief power in saving to the future the old church of Cranmer and Ridley was the Methodist revival. It broke upon the kingdom in tongues of flame. Then was the golden age of field preaching. In the venerable cathedrals of England the magnates of the church on the Lord's day preached to a dozen hearers; sometimes to less; occasionally to nobody but the sexton and the choir. An audience of two hundred was a crowd. At the same time Wesley and Whitefield were haranguing ten and twenty thousands at a time in the open air. The wisdom of the city fathers of Boston had not then illumined the world. The Church of England could no more withstand it than she could have withstood the day of judgment. To her it was the day of judgment. English Christianity has never lost the elements of spiritual life which Methodism, by direct reproof and by the power of contrast, then put into it. Methodism saved the Anglican Church from extinction. It was a reinforcement of apostolic Christianity, also, in every other Christian denomination in the English-speaking nations and colonies. We have all felt the throb of its pulsations. It has been what new blood is to falling dynasties and decadent races."

These are stronger terms than a Methodist could use with propriety, in giving to the readers of the NORTH AMERICAN REVIEW the reasons why he adheres to the faith and practice of John Wesley. Much is of course due to the conditions of birth and education in determining one's Christian associations. These conditions will at the least create a predisposition to accept for life one's hereditary faith. But no hereditary faith can permanently retain its hold upon a thoughtful man, unless it contains sufficient elements of truth to create positive convictions. It is a peculiarity of Methodists that they are what they are in religion *ex animo*; they are largely recruits to Christianity from the unchurched mass of the world. In the earlier days they were drawn also in great numbers from the other Protestant bodies. There has not been as yet, among Methodists, a sufficiency of time for the operation of the laws of hereditary influence to the extent which is common to other communions, whether Protestant or Catholic.

What, then, are the features of the great evangelical revival which endear it to all who have been brought by its power into the fellowship of the various Methodist churches? I think I may put in the forefront the fact that it draws so clear a distinction between opinion and religion. Here the Methodist would join hands with Edward Everett Hale in his presentation of the principles of Unitarianism in the March number of this Review. When Mr. Hale writes: "A simple and probable theology is a very good thing; just as a simple doctrine of attraction, or of electricity, or of evolution, is a very good thing; but religion, the life of man with God, or his infinite and immortal life, is a greater reality, and is the only reality for which our churches care,"

He almost repeats John Wesley himself. Wesley's expressions on this point are so habitual that they may be accepted as representing the substance of his thinking. Some of them are memorable. "I make" he says, "no opinion the term of union with any man. I think and let think. What I want is holiness of heart and life. They who have this are my brother, sister, and mother." And, rising to a height which the Christian world has not yet reached, he exclaims: "I desire to have a league, offensive and defensive, with every soldier of Christ." To another correspondent he writes: "Orthodoxy, or right opinion, is at best a very slender part of religion, if it can be allowed to be any part at all." His impatience of the substitution of doctrine for piety comes to an extreme statement in his declaration often quoted: "I am sick of opinions." He showed his catholicity in the publication of a biography of Thomas Firmin, one of the early propagators of Unitarianism in England, saying, as he did so, that he could not accept Firmin's doctrinal beliefs, but that he saw in him an example of Christian excellence worthy of imitation. And it was in harmony with this large hearted charity that he received, as his guest at his orphan house in Newcastle, a Roman Catholic priest, when Roman Catholic priests were, on political grounds, objects of suspicion. Not satisfied with this, he subsequently became the priest's guest, delivered a discourse in his chapel (part of an old Franciscan convent), and lived in friendship with him ever after. This habit of looking beyond opinion to the image of Christ in men was not only characteristic of Wesley himself, but became also one of the traits of the Methodist people. I cannot say, however, that they have always, in catholicity, quite equalled their founder.

Clearly, then, Wesley did not set out to found a church. If he had, he would have laid stress on opinions. He might then have defined and refined, until the substance of Christian truth had disappeared from ordinary human vision. Wesley's war was with practical ungodliness, and the simplest truths of the gospel were the weapons of his warfare. And what an England it was, into the midst of which he threw himself! One has only to read his journals to obtain a clearer impression of it than can be had from any historian of our day. Lecky tells us: "The passion for gin drinking appears to have infected the masses of the population, and it spread with the rapidity and the violence of an epidemic. Small as is the place which this fact occupies in English history, it was probably, if we consider all the consequences that have flowed from it, the most momentous in that of the eighteenth century—incomparably more so than any event in the purely political or military annals of the country. The fatal passion for drink was at once and irrevocably planted in the nation. The grand jury of Middlesex, in a powerful presentment, declared that much the greater part of the poverty, the murders, the robberies of London, might be traced to this single cause. Retailers of gin were accustomed to hang out painted boards announcing that their customers could be made drunk for a penny, and dead-drunk for two-pence, and should have straw for nothing; and cellars strewn with straw were accordingly provided, into which those who had become insensible were dragged, and where they remained till they had sufficiently recovered to renew their orgies. The evil acquired such frightful dimensions that even the unreforming Parliament of Walpole perceived the necessity of taking strong measures to arrest it." Thousands of the baptized members of the Church of England were no better. Wesley himself calls them as he saw them: "Drunken Christians, cursing and swearing Christians, lying Christians, cheating Christians," and adds, "If these are Christians at all, they are devil Christians, as the poor Malabarians term them."

Having found persons who sought his aid in escaping from the contagion of this wickedness, he appointed one evening of the week for meeting with them. From this small beginning the Methodist churches arose. It soon became necessary to frame terms of union by which these associated seekers after Christian truth and Christian life could be held together. The terms of union are known as the "General Rules of the United Societies." They are doctrinal by implication, but very little so by any express statement. As the basis of a church, they would be pronounced by any theologian wholly inadequate, and yet they are the basis of Methodism. And they suggest the thought that, perhaps, the best way to found a church is to found it more than we do on practical Christianity.

As most probably many of the readers of the NORTH AMERICAN REVIEW have not met with John Wesley's General Rules, they are given here entire. The life-blood of Methodism is in them. "There is one only condition previously required in those who desire admission into these societies: a desire to flee from the wrath to come and to be saved from their sins. But, wherever this is really fixed in the soul, it will be shown by its fruits. It is therefore expected of all who continue therein, that they should continue to evidence their desire of salvation: First, by doing no harm, by avoiding evil in every kind; especially that which is most generally practiced: such is, the taking the name of God in vain; the profaning the day of the Lord, either by doing ordinary work thereon, or by buying or selling; drunkenness, buying or selling spirituous liquors, or drinking them, unless in cases of extreme necessity; fighting, quarreling, brawling, brother going to law with brother, returning evil for evil, or railing for railing; the using many words in buying or selling; the buying or selling uncustomed goods; the giving or taking things on usury, that is, unlawful interest; uncharitable or unprofitable conversation, particularly speaking evil of magistrates or ministers; doing to others as we would not they should do unto us; doing what we know is not for the glory of God, as the 'putting on of gold and costly apparel'; the taking such diversions as cannot be used in the name of the Lord Jesus; the singing those songs, or reading those books, which do not tend to the knowledge or love of God; softness, and needless self-indulgence; laying up treasures upon earth; borrowing without a probability of paying; or taking up goods without a probability of paying for them.

"Secondly, by doing good, by being, in every kind, merciful after their power; as they have opportunity, doing good of every possible sort, and as far as is possible, to all men; to their bodies, of the ability which God giveth, by giving food to the hungry, by clothing the naked, by visiting or helping them that are sick or are in prison; to their souls, by instructing, reproving, or exhorting all they have any intercourse with; trampling under foot that enthusiastic doctrine of devils, that 'we are not to do good unless our heart be free to it'; by doing good especially to them that are of the household of faith, or groaning so to be; employing them preferably to others; buying one of another; helping each other in business; and so much the more, because the world will love its own, and them only; by all possible diligence and frugality, that the gospel be not blamed; by running with patience the race that is set before them, 'denying themselves, and taking up their cross daily'; submitting to bear the reproach of Christ, to be as the filth and off scouring of the world; and looking that, all men should 'say all manner of evil of them falsely for the Lord's sake.'

"Thirdly, by attending upon all the ordinances of God. Such are, the public worship of God; the ministry of the word, either read or expounded;

the supper of the Lord; family and private prayer; searching the scriptures; and fasting or abstinence.

"Men before Wesley have counseled their fellows to be good and have provided forms of discipline for making them better, and have conspicuously failed. Wesley was not so unschooled in the knowledge of human nature as to attempt to work without means. A decided Christian, he relied upon Christian truth as the animating energy of his reform of the people. How, then, did he conceive Christian truth? After depreciating so energetically mere opinion in religion, what were his own opinions? To say that he was without positive theological convictions would impeach his intelligence. A more positive man in thought and act never lived in England. To answer our question, we must look for a few minutes at the theology and the preaching of the English clergy in the eighteenth century. The gospel of the English divines of that period was the gospel of moderation; the preaching was the inculcation of morals. The prevalent theory of Christianity was that it was a republication of natural religion, accredited by the historic evidence of miracles. Paley said, that the only purpose of Christianity was to afford men a more certain assurance of a future life. The

Deists attacked the theologians by affirming that natural religion was enough, and pressed them very hard. As to the essence of religion, Deist and Christian were on the same ground; if the Deist did not care for the added evidence which Christianity was supposed to bring, he had no use for Christianity. As to the inner contents of religion he was as well off as priest, deacon, or bishop. Lecky, who is no evangelical, says that the theologians, who were contemporary with Wesley, "beyond a belief in the doctrine of the Trinity and a general acknowledgment of the gospel narratives, taught little that might not have been taught by the disciples of Socrates or Confucius. "Then, again, the struggles between Church men and Dissenters had ended in weariness of all theological strife. The theological passions, which had displaced true religious fervor, had worn themselves out. The Puritans had been terribly in earnest, and had overthrown the monarchy; therefore the Churchmen studied all the more assiduously to maintain the golden mean. Moderation, the avoidance of over-much righteousness, the danger of religious enthusiasm, were the stock phrases of the clergy. John Locke's "Reasonableness of Christianity," exactly suited the temper of his generation. And the clergy were moderate, very moderate indeed, in every sense of that epithet. The church was dying of inanition, and the people were going from bad to worse. As there was nothing left of Christianity to preach but its morality, morality was the staple of all the sermons. Be moral, be moral, sounded from all the pulpits of England on Sundays, and the answer came in the drunkenness and ferocity of the lower classes, and the gambling and fast living of the higher ranks of society. Bishop Butler's preface to his Analogy is one of the most melancholy passages in all eighteenth century literature: "It is come to be taken for granted by many persons that Christianity is now at length discovered to be fictitious; and, accordingly, they treat it as if, in the present age, this were an agreed point among all people of discernment, and nothing remained but to set it up as a principal subject of mirth and ridicule, as it were by way of reprisals, for its having so long interrupted the pleasures of the world." And all he will undertake to show is that "it is not so clear a case that there is nothing in it." And yet Butler distrusted Wesley and Wesley's work, and believed his zealous contemporary to be a propagator of dangerous religious enthusiasm.

To this listlessness of the pulpit and ungodliness of the people, Wesley opposed three truths which he believed to be drawn directly from the

New Testament: (1) Man is lost. (2) Man may be saved if he will. (3) He may be saved now, with a tremendous emphasis on the now. All this implies the mediation of Christ, and the direct action of the Holy Spirit upon the heart, applying and giving efficacy to the truths contained in the gospel. In other words, Wesley held that Christianity is a supernatural administration running through all ages, and that the administrator is the Holy Spirit. On this point he took issue with the theologians of England. He succeeded in indoctrinating his people with this thought, so that it has become and remains one of their deepest convictions, and as such is a vital force of Methodism. A Methodist is a supernaturalist of the most pronounced type. As it was said of the old Roman, *quod vult, valde vult*; so it may be said of every Methodist who is true to the teachings of his church, that what he believes he believes with all his soul.

I must not, however, stray too far into the realm of technical theology. This much, however, needed to be said, in order to show the difference between Methodism and the theology of the eighteenth century. The marking of this distinction helps also to make the inner life of Methodism clear to those who are not familiar with its principles. In showing how directly Wesley's teaching antagonized the opinions of the leading theologians of the eighteenth century, I prefer to cite other than Methodist testimony. I apprehend that Methodists are thought by many candid persons to claim too much for the revolution wrought by their fathers in the religious life and thought of the English-speaking race, and that, therefore, their assertions on this point are usually accepted with a good many grains of disbelief. I will, therefore, take Hunt, whose "History of Religious Thought in England" is eminently fair to all parties. Hunt makes the point that the English scholars having, with great difficulty, beaten back the Deists on the grounds of argument which they chose, found that "Wesley and Whitefield were attracting to the churches crowds of people who professed to realize in themselves the truth of that religion which the Deists were said to have assailed. Dr. Waterland was the first to see the danger of the rising sect. He did not condescend to name them, but wrote against them as the 'New Enthusiasts.' The Methodists really told the people that they must be born again before they could enter the kingdom of God, and Dr. Waterland proved that they had all been born again in baptism, and were already members of Christ and inheritors of

His kingdom." Of course, the Methodist preaching was a scandal and offense to all refined England. The claim of the direct action of the Holy Spirit upon the soul seemed to men, who were undoubtedly sincere, to open the door to all possibilities of extravagance. "That the Spirit of God," adds Hunt, "had virtually departed from the world was a doctrine universally received both by Churchmen and Dissenters. The theory was that in the first ages of Christianity the Spirit had gone with the Apostles working miracles, and that in virtue of these miracles Christianity was believed. After a time the Spirit withdrew from the church and miracles ceased. The Bible, or according to another theory, the church, took the place of the Spirit. "As this was the feature of Methodism which most aroused the opposition of English clergymen of the last century, it is well to accumulate evidences of their opposition. The doctrine of the direct action of the Spirit on man is connected in evangelical theology with the kindred doctrine of immediate justification by faith. The immediacy of pardon carries with it (according to this theology) the comforting assurance of peace through the gift of the same Spirit. Lavington, Bishop of Exeter, denied, as against Wesley and Whitefield, that men are justified by faith alone. "When our church," says this bishop, "affirms our being justified or saved by faith alone, as distinguished from the works of the law, or mere moral righteousness, it means such a faith as worketh by love; faith including good works, or in conjunction with them." Thus we have an English bishop who does not know better than to define justification in the terms of the Council of Trent. "For 'faith,'" says the council, "unless hope and love are added thereto, neither unites man perfectly with Christ nor makes him a living member of his body." And a critic of Methodism, in the London Examiner of that period, bears testimony to the prevalence of this opinion among theologians. "It is not easy," says this writer, "to discern what any of the Methodists mean by the salvation of faith without works. The most learned theologians, in their explanation of the word faith, are generally agreed that there is no such salvation." And Warburton, scandalized by some alleged instances of conversion, says of them in his coarse fashion: "The devil was here only in the office of man-midwife to the new birth." This will do very well for "the book-laden Warburton," the most wooden of Shakespearean critics, who could twist the theology of Pope's "Essay on Man" into some sort of conformity with Christianity, but who certainly never comprehended his New Testament. And last of all, the Examiner critic, already named, lights up his censure of Methodism with a slight gleam of humor when he describes the Methodists as "the refuse of society, claiming familiarity with all the persons of the Trinity, and talking of going to heaven as they would of the one-shilling gallery."

Enough has been said, perhaps more than enough, to make it clear: (1) That original Methodism was in direct conflict with the theology dominant in England at the time. (2) That it was a restatement of the early reformation doctrine of justification by faith alone, and its effect upon the human soul, peace with God. Mr. Wesley persistently declared that these doctrines are contained in the articles of the Church of England, as they certainly were; but they had been obscured, by the glosses of the theologians, till their meaning was lost. We can see, too, in what sense Wesley said that he was "sick of opinions." He was sick of opinions which were offered as substitutes for character, which were not used as means of carrying a new and divine life to men. His clear and logical mind could not be satisfied with less than precisely defined opinions. He first, however, submitted all his thoughts to the authority of the Bible; and next he laid stress on those doctrines only which in his view ministered to life. "Life is more than dogma" is the triumphing and triumphant assertion of Methodism. And in that, Methodists believe, is the beginning of the renovation of modern theology. Dogma is of importance chiefly as it ministers to life; beyond, the sphere of life it is important mainly as opinion. As opinion, it maybe inexpressibly precious to the thinking mind, but as such it ought not to be forced upon the consciences of all and sundry, at the peril of their salvation if refused. Methodism has a distinctly defined theology, but it is chiefly concerned with that part of theology which mediates salvation to the human soul. Yet in all its thinking, it submits every opinion, as Wesley did, to the authority of the revealed word. It does not make the Christian consciousness the judge of what is divine and what not divine in Scripture; contrarily, it makes Scripture the test of the purity and reality of the Christian consciousness.

It remains now to speak briefly of the effects of Methodism upon modern society, as reason, in addition to its spirit, why one is a Methodist. It is not necessary here to recount statistically its successes. For myself, I have a disrelish for the parade of statistics, which tell us of so many churches, so many ministers and members, so much of this and that, to the end of the chapter. Great aggregates are not incompatible with decay, as the condition of the Church of England at the time of the rise of Methodism shows. I will, therefore, turn aside from Methodist eulogy, of which we have an abundance in these days, and let others speak for us. Lecky makes for Methodism two claims: first, that it saved England from convulsion during the time of the French Revolution, and again that, in these days of vast aggregations of capital, it stands between the rich and the poor. These are important statements, if true; but let us hear our witness. After an eloquent description of the intoxicating power of French revolutionary ideas upon the masses of the English people, Lecky says: "England on the whole escaped the contagion. Many causes conspired to save her, but among them a prominent place must, I believe, be given to the new and vehement religious enthusiasm which was at that very time passing through the middle and lower classes of the people, which had enlisted in its service a large proportion of the wilder and more impetuous reformers, and which recoiled with horror from the anti-Christian tenets that were associated with revolution in France." And his testimony on the next point, the widening chasm between the rich and poor, is most apposite to our own times. "Any change of conditions which widens the chasm and impairs the sympathy between rich and poor cannot fail, however beneficial may be its other effects, to bring with it grave dangers to the State. It is incontestable that the immense increase of manufacturing industry and of the manufacturing population has had this tendency; and it is, therefore, particularly fortunate, that it should have been preceded by a religious revival which opened a new spring of moral and religious energy among the poor, and at the same time gave a powerful impulse to the philanthropy of the rich."

I wish I could claim for Methodism in America all that Lecky here asserts of it, as a mediator between the rich and the poor. This much, however, may be confidently asserted, that should the supreme trial of our institutions ever come, it will be found that Methodism has done its full share toward preparing the people to meet the shock of the trial with the firmness of Christian men. It will be seen then, that the plain gospellers—Methodist and other—who have performed their work in obscurity, have trained the masses of the nation in moral thoughtfulness, in reverence for law, in the courage which counts no sacrifice too great for the maintenance of civil and social order. A church of the common people, Methodism will be found invaluable to the State here. *I am a Methodist because I believe*

Methodism to be the recovery of the original spirit of the Protestant reformation. The feuds between Lutheran and Reformed on the Continent, and between Churchman and Dissenter in England, had changed the revival of religion, which Luther brought in, into a revival of theological polemics. The head usurped the place of the heart, the rage for orthodoxy drove out zeal for piety, and faith in the creed was made the substitute for personal faith in Christ. Methodism, as I believe, has brought the Protestant reformation to its true path again. I am a Methodist because I conceive that the true test of a Christian Church is its power with the common people; and Methodism bears this test. As the reformation of the individual proceeds from within outward, so the reformation of society proceeds from beneath upward. *I am a Methodist, therefore, because I think that, in this regard, Methodism is in the right line of progress, and follows the procedure of original Christianity.* The uncommon people in this world are a small minority; what is needed is a faith that can sit down as a friend at the humblest fireside, that can be the companion of the lowly in their struggles with want and sin, that can bring cheer to souls that have little else to cheer them: and such a faith Methodism has been. I hope it will preserve this most precious trait of character; for it is a strong reason, why, passing by other churches in which I see so much to love, I am yet a Methodist.

George B. Crooks,

ABOUT CROSSREACH PUBLICATIONS

Thank you for choosing CrossReach Publications.

Hope. Inspiration. Trust.

These three words sum up the philosophy of why CrossReach Publications exist. To create inspiration for the present thus inspiring hope for the future, through trusted authors from previous generations.

We are *non-denominational* and *non-sectarian.* We appreciate and respect what every part of the body brings to the table and believe everyone has the right to study and come to their own conclusions. We aim to help facilitate that end.

We aspire to excellence. If we have not met your standards please contact us and let us know. We want you to feel satisfied with your product. Something for everyone. We publish quality books both in presentation and content from a wide variety of authors who span various doctrinal positions and traditions, on a wide variety of Christian topics that will teach, encourage, challenge, inspire and equip.

We're a family-based home-business. A husband and wife team raising 8 kids. If you have any questions or comments about our publications email us at:

ContactUs@CrossReach.net

Don't forget you can follow us on Facebook and Twitter, (links are on the copyright page above) to keep up to date on our newest titles and deals.

BESTSELLING TITLES FROM CROSSREACH[1]

How to Be Filled with the Holy Spirit
A. W. Tozer

Before we deal with the question of how to be filled with the Holy Spirit, there are some matters which first have to be settled. As believers you have to get them out of the way, and right here is where the difficulty arises. I have been afraid that my listeners might have gotten the idea somewhere that I had a how-to-be-filled-with-the-Spirit-in-five-easy-lessons doctrine, which I could give you. If you can have any such vague ideas as that, I can only stand before you and say, "I am sorry"; because it isn't true; I can't give you such a course. There are some things, I say, that you have to get out of the way, settled.

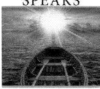

God Still Speaks
A. W. Tozer

Tozer is as popular today as when he was living on the earth. He is respected right across the spectrum of Christianity, in circles that would disagree sharply with him doctrinally. Why is this? A. W. Tozer was a man who knew the voice of God. He shared this experience with every true child of God. With all those who are called by the grace of God to share in the mystical union that is possible with Him through His Son Jesus.

Tozer fought against much dryness and formality in his day. Considered a mighty man of God by most Evangelicals today, he was unconventional in his approach to spirituality and had no qualms about consulting everyone from Catholic Saints to German Protestant mystics for inspiration on how to experience God more fully.

Tozer, just like his Master, doesn't fit neatly into our theological boxes. He was a man after God's own heart and was willing to break the rules (man-made ones that is) to get there.

Here are two writings by Tozer that touch on the heart of this goal. Revelation is Not Enough and The Speaking Voice. A bonus chapter The Menace of the Religious Movie is included.

This is meat to sink your spiritual teeth into. Tozer's writings will show you the way to satisfy your spiritual hunger.

What We Are in Christ

E. W. Kenyon

I was surprised to find that the expressions "in Christ," "in whom," and "in Him" occur more than 130 times in the New Testament. This is the heart of the Revelation of Redemption given to Paul. Here is the secret of faith—faith that conquers, faith that moves mountains. Here is the secret of the Spirit's guiding us into all reality. The heart craves intimacy with the Lord Jesus and with the Father. This craving can now be satisfied.

Ephesians 1:7: "In whom we have our redemption through his blood, the remission of our trespasses according to the riches of his grace."

It is not a beggarly Redemption, but a real liberty in Christ that we have now. It is a Redemption by the God Who could say, "Let there be lights in the firmament of heaven," and cause the whole starry heavens to leap into being in a single instant. It is Omnipotence beyond human reason. This is where philosophy has never left a footprint.

Claiming Our Rights
E. W. Kenyon

There is no excuse for the spiritual weakness and poverty of the Family of God when the wealth of Grace and Love of our great Father with His power and wisdom are all at our disposal. We are not coming to the Father as a tramp coming to the door begging for food; we come as sons not only claiming our legal rights but claiming the natural rights of a child that is begotten in love. No one can hinder us or question our right of approach to our Father. Satan has Legal Rights over the sinner that God cannot dispute or challenge. He can sell them as slaves; he owns them, body, soul and spirit. But the moment we are born again... receive Eternal Life, the nature of God,—his legal dominion ends.

Christ is the Legal Head of the New Creation, or Family of God, and all the Authority that was given Him, He has given us: (Matthew 28:18), "All authority in heaven," the seat of authority, and "on earth," the place of execution of authority. He is "head over all things," the highest authority in the Universe, for the benefit of the Church which is His body.

The Two Babylons
Alexander Hislop

Fully Illustrated High Res. Images. Complete and Unabridged.
Expanded Seventh Edition. This is the first and only seventh edition available in a modern digital edition. Nothing is left out! New material not found in the first six editions!!!

Available in eBook and paperback edition exclusively from CrossReach Publications.

There is this great difference between the works of men and the works of God, that the same minute and searching investigation, which displays the defects and imperfections of the one, brings out also the beauties of the other. If the most finely polished needle on which the art of man has been expended be subjected to a microscope, many inequalities, much roughness and clumsiness, will be seen. But if the microscope be brought to bear on the flowers of the field, no such result appears. Instead of their beauty diminishing, new beauties and still more delicate, that have escaped the naked eye, are forthwith discovered; beauties that make us appreciate, in a way which otherwise we could have had little conception of, the full force of the Lord's saying, "Consider the lilies of the field, how they grow; they toil not, neither do they spin: and yet I say unto you, That even Solomon, in all his glory, was not arrayed like one of these." The same law appears also in comparing the Word of God and the most finished productions of men. There are spots and blemishes in the most admired productions of human genius. But the more the Scriptures are searched, the more minutely they are studied, the more their perfection appears; new beauties are brought into light every day; and the discoveries of science, the researches of the learned, and the labours of infidels, all alike conspire to illustrate the wonderful harmony of all the parts, and the Divine beauty that clothes the whole. If this be the case with Scripture in general, it is especially the case with prophetic Scripture. As every spoke in the wheel of Providence revolves, the prophetic symbols start into still more bold and beautiful relief. This is very strikingly the case with the prophetic language that forms the groundwork and cornerstone of the present work. There never has been any difficulty in the mind of any enlightened Protestant in identifying the woman "sitting on seven mountains," and having on her forehead the name written, "Mystery, Babylon the Great," with the Roman apostacy.

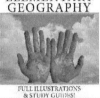

Elementary Geography
Charlotte Mason

This little book is confined to very simple "reading lessons upon the Form and Motions of the Earth, the Points of the Compass, the Meaning of a Map: Definitions."
It is hoped that these reading lessons may afford intelligent teaching, even in the hands of a young teacher.
Children should go through the book twice, and should, after the second reading, be able to answer any of the questions from memory.

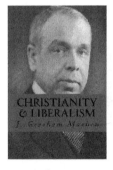

Christianity and Liberalism
J. Gresham Machen

The purpose of this book is not to decide the religious issue of the present day, but merely to present the issue as sharply and clearly as possible, in order that the reader may be aided in deciding it for himself. Presenting an issue sharply is indeed by no means a popular business at the present time; there are many who prefer to fight their intellectual battles in what Dr. Francis L. Patton has aptly called a "condition of low visibility." Clear-cut definition of terms in religious matters, bold facing of the logical implications of religious views, is by many persons regarded as an impious proceeding. May it not discourage contribution to mission boards? May it not hinder the progress of consolidation, and produce a poor showing in columns of Church statistics? But with such persons we cannot possibly bring ourselves to agree. Light may seem at times to be an impertinent intruder, but it is always beneficial in the end. The type of religion which rejoices in the pious sound of traditional phrases, regardless of their meanings, or shrinks from "controversial" matters, will never stand amid the shocks of life. In the sphere of religion, as in other spheres, the things about which men are agreed are apt to be the things that are least worth holding; the really important things are the things about which men will fight.

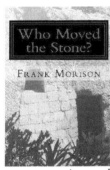

Who Moved the Stone?
Frank Morison

This study is in some ways so unusual and provocative that the writer thinks it desirable to state here very briefly how the book came to take its present form. In one sense it could have taken no other, for it is essentially a confession, the inner story of a man who originally set out to write one kind of book and found himself compelled by the sheer force of circumstances to write another.

It is not that the facts themselves altered, for they are recorded imperishably in the monuments and in the pages of human history. But the interpretation to be put upon the facts underwent a change. Somehow the perspective shifted—not suddenly, as in a flash of insight or inspiration, but slowly, almost imperceptibly, by the very stubbornness of the facts themselves.

The book as it was originally planned was left high and dry, like those Thames barges when the great river goes out to meet the incoming sea. The writer discovered one day that not only could he no longer write the book as he had once conceived it, but that he would not if he could.

To tell the story of that change, and to give the reasons for it, is the main purpose of the following pages.

The Person and Work of the Holy Spirit
R. A. Torey

Before one can correctly understand the work of the Holy Spirit, he must first of all know the Spirit Himself. A frequent source of error and fanaticism about the work of the Holy Spirit is the attempt to study and understand His work without first of all coming to know Him as a Person.

It is of the highest importance from the standpoint of worship that we decide whether the Holy Spirit is a Divine Person, worthy to receive our adoration, our faith, our love, and our entire surrender to Himself, or whether it is simply an influence emanating from God or a power or an illumination that God imparts to us. If the Holy Spirit is a person, and a Divine Person, and we do not know Him as such, then we are robbing a Divine Being of the worship and the faith and the love and the surrender to Himself which are His due.

In His Steps
Charles M. Sheldon

The sermon story, In His Steps, or "What Would Jesus Do?" was first written in the winter of 1896, and read by the author, a chapter at a time, to his Sunday evening congregation in the Central Congregational Church, Topeka, Kansas. It was then printed as a serial in The Advance (Chicago), and its reception by the readers of that paper was such that the publishers of The Advance made arrangements for its appearance in book form. It was their desire, in which the author heartily joined, that the story might reach as many readers as possible, hence succeeding editions of paper-covered volumes at a price within the reach of nearly all readers.

The story has been warmly and thoughtfully welcomed by Endeavor societies, temperance organizations, and Y. M. C. A. 's. It is the earnest prayer of the author that the book may go its way with a great blessing to the churches for the quickening of Christian discipleship, and the hastening of the Master's kingdom on earth.

Charles M. Sheldon.
Topeka, Kansas,
November, 1897.

Made in United States
Troutdale, OR
11/09/2023

14407453R00022